A ROOKIE BIOGRAPHY

ELIZABETH BLACKWELL

First Woman Doctor

By Carol Greene

 CHILDRENS PRESS®

CHICAGO

This book is for Meredith Toole.

Elizabeth Blackwell (1821-1910)

Library of Congress Cataloging-in-Publication Data

Greene, Carol.
    Elizabeth Blackwell : first woman doctor / by Carol Greene.
      p. cm. — (A Rookie biography)
    Summary: A biography of the first woman doctor in the United States,
who worked in both America and England to open the field of medicine
to women.
    ISBN 0-516-04217-3
    1. Blackwell, Elizabeth, 1821-1910—Juvenile literature. 2. Women
physicians—United States—Juvenile literature. [1. Blackwell, Elizabeth,
1821-1910. 2. Women physicians. 3. Physicians.] I. Title. II. Series: Greene,
Carol. Rookie biography.
R154.B623G74   1991
610'.92—dc20
[B]
[92]   90-20001
                                    CIP
                                      AC

Elizabeth Blackwell
was a real person.
She was born in 1821.
She died in 1910.
After many hard times,
Elizabeth Blackwell became
the first woman doctor.
This is her story.

✦✦

TABLE OF CONTENTS

Elizabeth Blackwell was born in Bristol, England.

Chapter 1

Little Shy

Elizabeth never said much.
She was so quiet that
Papa called her "Little Shy."
But Elizabeth thought
and Elizabeth worried
—a lot.

She worried about being
a really good girl.
Would sleeping on the floor
make her really good?
Elizabeth tried that.
It didn't work.

Elizabeth worried about
getting married too.
What if she never did?
Back then, unmarried women
had a terrible time.

They could teach, sew,
or be servants.
Unmarried women often
had to live in other
people's houses.
They were very poor.

Servants worked in the
homes of rich people.
They did all the work
of the household,
including styling
hair (left) and
serving food (above).

But sometimes Elizabeth
was too busy to worry.
She liked to read.
She liked to take walks
and to play with her
eight sisters and brothers.

Most of all, Elizabeth
liked to learn.
Papa hired good teachers
for his children.

The Blackwell family
came to America in
a ship like this one.

When Elizabeth was 11,
her family moved
from England to America.
The boat trip took
seven and a half weeks.
Elizabeth was seasick.

When the Blackwells moved there, New York was crowded and dirty. Many people lived in slums (left). Can you see the pigs in the street scene above?

At first, she didn't like America very much. The Blackwell family lived in an ugly house in New York City. Pigs roamed the streets.

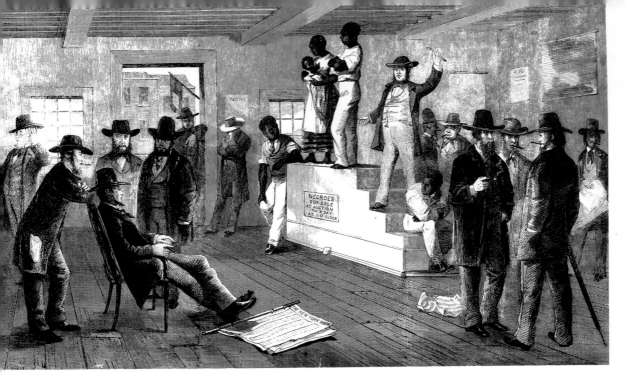

Slaves were bought and sold like any other property.

Worst of all, in some parts
of America, white people
owned black people.
This was called slavery.
Papa hated it
and so did Elizabeth.

Later, the Blackwells
moved to New Jersey.
But Elizabeth went
to school in New York.

She still liked learning
—all but one class.
It was about bodies.
Bodies and sickness
made Elizabeth feel sick.

Elizabeth grew to be
a strong, smart girl.
But she was still
small and shy and
she still worried a lot.

Now Elizabeth worried about
what to do with her life.
She wanted to do
something important.
But she was a girl.
What *could* she do?

Cincinnati in the 1850s. Steam-powered riverboats
stopped at this big city on the Ohio River.

Chapter 2

A Strange Idea

Her family moved
to Cincinnati, Ohio.
What a beautiful town!
thought Elizabeth.
Maybe she could do
something important there.

But three months later,
Papa died. Now the
Blackwells were poor.

Even in America, women couldn't do much to make money, except teach, sew, be a servant, or work in a factory.

Jobs for women in the nineteenth century mostly involved making and sewing cloth. They worked long hours for low wages in crowded factories.

At first, Elizabeth thought that it was
a strange idea for her to become a doctor.

The Blackwells started
a school in their home.
Elizabeth hated teaching,
but she did it anyway.

Then one day she visited
a sick friend, Mary.
Mary said that she
would not feel so bad
if she had a woman doctor.

Why don't you become a doctor?
she asked Elizabeth.
You would be a good one.
Promise to think about it.

Elizabeth promised.
But what a strange idea!
Women couldn't be doctors.
Besides, bodies and sickness
made her feel sick.

But Mary's strange idea
would not go away.
Somebody had to be
the first woman doctor.
Why not Elizabeth?

At last she decided.
She would try.
She would teach,
save money, and study
with other doctors.
Then she would go
to school.

Twenty-nine medical schools
rejected Elizabeth, but
she kept trying.

Elizabeth worked for two years.
She had to leave home.
That was hard.
Once she felt as if
her heart would break.
"Help me!" she prayed.

Then she felt God with her
and knew she was doing
the right thing.
Bodies and sickness didn't
make her feel sick anymore.
Bodies were beautiful.

Most medical schools
didn't want a woman.
Twenty-nine schools said no.
But Elizabeth kept trying.
Then little Geneva College
in New York said yes.

Geneva Medical College in Geneva, New York, accepted
Elizabeth Blackwell as the first woman medical student.

On November 4, 1847,
Elizabeth left for Geneva.
At last she would be
doing something important.

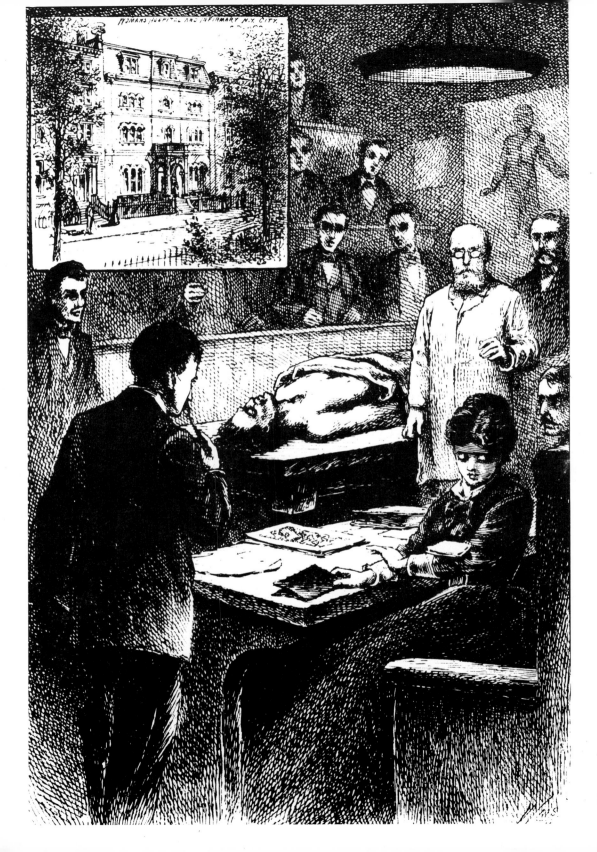

Doctor Blackwell

Many people thought Elizabeth
would never make it
through medical school.
Some called her crazy.
Some called her bad.

But she worked hard.
The men students liked her.
They were always polite.

**Doctor Blackwell learned as much as
she could in medical school.**

Elizabeth graduated from medical school in 1849.

On January 23, 1849,
Elizabeth graduated
first in her class.
She was Dr. Blackwell now,
the first woman doctor.

Chapter 3

Blackwell's diploma from Geneva Medical College (above) was written in Latin. Dr. Benjamin Hale, president of the college (left), awarded her the diploma.

23

A street in Paris, France

Elizabeth wanted to learn more,
so she went to Paris, France,
to work in a hospital.
But no hospital wanted her,
because she was a woman.

24

At last, a hospital
for mothers and babies
said she could study there.
It was noisy, dirty, and hard.
But Elizabeth learned
and she was happy.

Newborn babies were kept warm in "incubators"
at a Paris hospital for mothers and babies.

Then she caught
a disease in her eye.
She couldn't see.
She couldn't work.
It was a terrible time.

Months went by.
Then a doctor took out
her sick eye and
gave her a glass one.
Her other eye grew strong
and she could work again.

Elizabeth Blackwell worked and studied at
St. Bartholomew's Hospital in London, England.

Elizabeth went to
a big hospital in London.
She made new friends
and learned new things.

27

Conditions in nineteenth-century hospitals were terrible.
Rats ran over patients at a New York hospital (above).
Doctors wore their street clothes (below) and did not
wash their hands between patients.

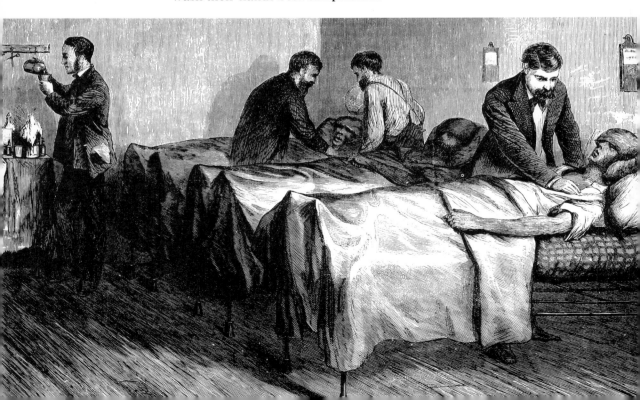

Back then, hospitals
were dirty places.
Nothing got washed,
not even doctors' hands.

Doctor Blackwell
in London, wearing
a coat called
the "doctorial sack"

Elizabeth began to think
that was wrong.
More people would get well
if things were clean.
Maybe she could change that.

But first she would change
her own life again.
She would go back
to New York City.
That was where she
could do the most good.

Chapter 4

Work

At first, people would not
go to a woman doctor.
But Elizabeth knew
who really needed her—
poor women and children.

Poor women in New York City were served free meals at the St. Barnabas Home.

Sick people wait for free medicine at a charity drugstore.

So she opened an office
where they could come
and be treated for free.
Some friends paid for it.

Elizabeth told her patients
they must eat good food,
rest, and keep clean.
Then they'd be healthy.
She made speeches
about staying healthy, too.

Back then, many poor children
had no mother or father.
They were orphans.
Elizabeth took an orphan girl,
Kitty, to live with her.

Soon Kitty was *her* child.
She loved Elizabeth and
called her "My Doctor."

Thousands of poor and orphaned children lived and slept in the streets.

The Beekman Downtown Hospital in New York, 1857. The figure in black and white at the left is thought to be Elizabeth Blackwell.

Then Elizabeth's sister,
Emily, became a doctor, too.
In 1857, Elizabeth, Emily,
and a Polish woman, Dr. Zak,
opened a hospital for
poor women and children.

Other women could study
to be nurses at the hospital.
It was the first school
for nurses in America.

The New York Infirmary for Women
in New York (above). Elizabeth
Blackwell opened the
infirmary in 1857. Doctor
Blackwell's nursing
students (right) receive
a lesson in bandaging.

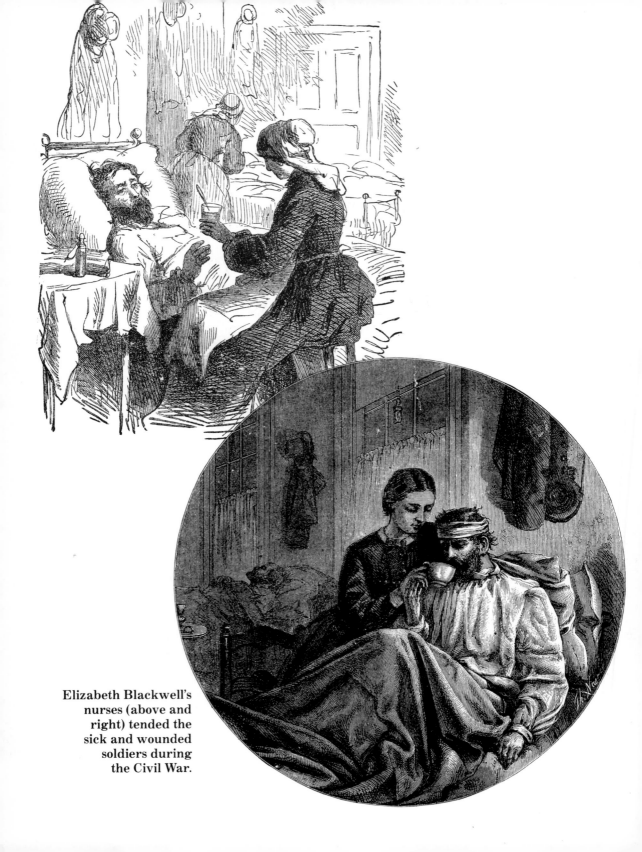

Elizabeth Blackwell's nurses (above and right) tended the sick and wounded soldiers during the Civil War.

President
Abraham
Lincoln

In 1860, Abraham Lincoln
became president, and
in 1861, the Civil War began.
It would end slavery,
and Elizabeth was glad.

She sent many nurses
to help the soldiers.
In 1864, she went
to Washington, D.C.,
and met President Lincoln.

By then, Elizabeth was sure
her ideas were right.
In 1865, her hospital
treated 31,657 people.
Only five died.
Keeping things clean *did* help.

In 1868, Elizabeth added
a medical college for
women to her hospital.
She taught the classes
about keeping things clean
and staying healthy.

Doctor Blackwell returned to England, where she helped
found the London School of Medicine for Women.

Then she knew her work
in America was done.
Her sister Emily could run
the school and hospital.

It was time for Elizabeth
to go back to England.

Student nurses
gather around
a patient (above).
Elizabeth Blackwell
(left) in the 1870s.

Chapter 5

Something Important

Back in England,
Elizabeth fought.

She fought for women doctors.
She fought for cleanliness
and for better care for
poor women and children.

Elizabeth wrote books
and made speeches.
She and two other women
started a medical school
for women in London.
Elizabeth taught there.

Elizabeth Blackwell (above left) and Kitty with their pet dogs. Elizabeth's younger brother, Henry Blackwell (left), was a speaker for women's rights.

42

In 1871, she started the
National Health Society.
It helped people learn
how to stay healthy.

Through all those years,
Kitty stayed with Elizabeth.
She took care of "My Doctor"
when Elizabeth grew
old and sick.

Today, women doctors are active at all levels of the medical profession.

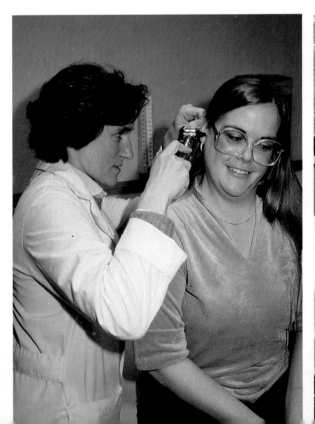

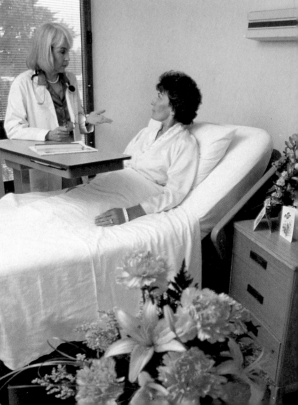

Elizabeth Blackwell opened
the medical profession to
women. She led the way
to fine modern hospitals
such as this one in
Houston, Texas

Elizabeth Blackwell
died in England
on May 31, 1910.
She was 89 years old.

The shy little girl
who worried about doing
something important
had done many important things
and helped many people.

Important Dates

1821   February 3—Born in Bristol, England, to Samuel and Hannah Blackwell

1832   Moved to United States

1838   Moved to Cincinnati, Ohio

1849   Graduated from Geneva Medical College in Geneva, New York

Studied in Paris, France

1853   Opened dispensary for poor women and children in New York City

1857   Opened hospital for poor women and children along with America's first training school for nurses in New York City

1868   Opened medical school for women

1869   Moved back to England

1871   Organized National Health Society

1910   May 31—Died in Hastings, England

INDEX

Page numbers in boldface type indicate illustrations.

PHOTO CREDITS

ABOUT THE AUTHOR

Carol Greene has degrees in English literature and musicology. She has worked in international exchange programs, as an editor, and as a teacher. She now lives in St. Louis, Missouri, and writes full-time. She has published more than eighty books. Others in the Rookie Biographies series include *Hans Christian Andersen, Ludwig van Beethoven, Black Elk, Daniel Boone, Christopher Columbus, Jacques Cousteau, Elizabeth the First, Benjamin Franklin, Martin Luther King, Jr., Robert E. Lee, Abraham Lincoln, John Muir, Louis Pasteur, Pocahontas, Jackie Robinson, George Washington*, and *Laura Ingalls Wilder*.